JUST ASK KIKY

A Single Parent's Guide to Surviving Being Broke and Having a Social Life

Nickiya Brown

DEDICATION

Giving GLORY to GOD for giving me the foundation to attempt to create something of my very own.
Thank you to my husband and love for life, Clayton for being supportive.
To Aijaye, Ayinde and the new Aaliyah for motivation to try again. Mommy loves you all!
Thank you to all my family and friends, especially those who helped me edit the first version.
Thanks for that much needed kick in the butt... lol!

Published by:
Nickiya Brown
P.O. Box 681316
Indianapolis, IN 46268
(317)824-9075
http://www.justaskkiky.com

ISBN: 9780692571279

Library of Congress Control Number: 2015920301

Layout Design by Cynthia Martin-Roper of nVision International www.nVisionInt.com

TABLE OF CONTENTS

INTRODUCTION

I'm broke. What can I do?

When I was a single mom of two, funds were always tight. In order to keep my sanity, I found family-friendly things that I could do within my budget. That means all things that are in the monetary range of FREE to FREE; well sometimes there was a small fee involved. I'm now married with a new little one so the need to save money has not changed.

What can you do for FREE? Funny you should ask, because you can do a whole lot more than you think!

Where to Look?

How to Look?

How to find what I found?

My first rule in finding FREE things to do is ...
LOOK AT EVERYTHING!

What does that mean? Literature is everywhere. It's posted on walls, in pamphlets, handouts, mailers, etc. You may say, well of course it is. Isn't that what advertisers are supposed to do? How many of you honestly read this material?

Most FREE things are not advertised on TV or radio commercials, so you have to search and re-search. Take for instance my local news mailer, shopLocal, which comes in Indiana residents' mailboxes at least once a week. These mailers look like a newspaper a few pages thick and hold the weekly advertisements from national and local retailer chains (Wal-Mart, Target, etc). They are easy to discard but don't throw them away. They often showcase events around town that are low cost or FREE to the public,; not to mention the recipes and restaurants that may be offering a promotion for that week. The next step is to check to see if there is a website. You can find what else is offered and some additional discounts. ShopLocal covers more than Indiana and they have online coupons (www.shoplocal.com).

My best finds are listed in the library. It's usually FREE to post information on library billboards as long as it doesn't include offensive content. Many organizations use this avenue of advertising. You can always find a free publication section somewhere in your local library. Scan through all the items displayed in this area. There are usually posters close by and some libraries separate documents based on subject, ex: educational material, FREE magazines/newspapers, non-profit groups' classes/events, etc. The point is to check out these sections thoroughly. There is a wealth of information to be found in these areas. Usually there is something that you can take with you. You can research those options that appeal to you further to make sure the event/class is something that will be a benefit to you and your family.

Several years ago, my children and I were taking classes at the Urban Arts Consortium (no longer in existence). Being that it was near the end of the summer and regular school would soon be back in session, my mind was on my upcoming need for an affordable aftercare program for my children. I had to find something...and quick. After class one day I just so happened to browse through information on a table in the entryway of the building. I noticed that it showcased marketing materials for many different types of businesses that were in some way related to each other or shared a similar theme. I never would have thought it, but I found a great after care program that was in my price range and close to my home. Can you imagine? I found it right there on that table. The point is that great resources are everywhere, so don't be afraid to look in those so-called obscure places.

Check the bulletin boards at your local grocery stores and small cafés. Starbucks and Half Price Books are great places to start looking for great events happening in the community.

Those FREE publications can be golden also. There are several around town geared towards all types of demographics which will usually highlight events that cater to that demographic living in the area. As mentioned before, these are not only posted in local libraries but also in newspaper stands on the street and in the lobby of small businesses.

Are you computer savvy? Mass emails, twitters, social postings and groups can also be a great resource. If you are computer savvy, you can find a lot of information on line. As a side note, please be careful with downloads from unfamiliar sources. Please check to ensure that it is a trusted source. I always search for an on-line imprint of a source I find. Since the web reaches a broader audience than print you will find additional deals and opportunities you may not find in the written publications.

The next time you see a table or wall filled with literature, take a look, you never know what you may find!

While many of my suggestions will focus around my hometown of Indianapolis, Indiana, I try to cover many events all over the country. The main point is that the techniques can be used in any town, anywhere. I hope this guide will help you find a few things that you and your children can enjoy together.

READING IS FUNDAMENTAL

My most favorite and fun FREE place to be any day of the week is the local library. The library is a plethora of fascinating worlds. So much is inside of a book.

The other great thing about the library is that there is always something going on for FREE. You can see movies, kids can play with computers for their age group; there are seminars; reading programs, and fun summer prize programs for young avid readers.

Many libraries have a pretty current stock of movies to rent for FREE with your library card. Depending on the library's budget, if they don't have something you want you can request they purchase it. That goes for books and movies. Ask a librarian for details. Be mindful of past due fees.

The library is also conveniently accessible via city bus lines and close to schools and community centers. Also a key thing to note is the abundance of other FREE activities in the surrounding area advertised in the FREE publications located at the front of most local libraries. You never know what you will find until you look.

To find out more about what the library has to offer, talk to a librarian or visit your local libraries website:www.publiclibraries.com/

Below are a few national programs to consider. Many are accessible in most school systems and in work conjunction with a public library.

Earn FREE Books!

Scholastic Inc. has several warehouses across the country. About four times a year they host major book fairs to reduce inventory. They offer crafts along with books for all ages, including adults, for up to 80% off and some as low as $1. They have a build a box deal which allows you to place as many of a specific set of books and items in a specific sized box for a certain fee, usually around $30. It may vary sale to sale. As long as the chosen items cannot fall out of the box it's all yours for that low low price.

The great find with this company is that if you are near one of the warehouses, they employ volunteers to help with the sale. Volunteers are paid in credit (not cash) towards the purchase of books at a hefty $10 in credits per hour. This is a great way to stock up on gifts or just fill your bookshelf for yourself and your kids. Visit www2.scholastic.com/ for more details.

Earn Prizes!

The library is not the only place where you can earn prizes for reading. Sylvan Learning Center sponsors the http://www.bookadventure.org website. Book Adventure is a FREE motivational reading program on-line to get your young one's in gear. Basically children in grades K-8 can choose to read from a provided list of 7000 books. They then take a quiz showing that they actually read or listened to the book and earn points for great prizes. The site has great links to resources for kids, parents, and teachers too.

Book Clubs

Have a teen that is into books? Teenreads.com is an online site where teens can discuss books, learn about starting a book club and find out about new titles and their authors. The site is a member of The Book Report Network, a group of websites founded in 1996 that share thoughtful book reviews, compelling features, in-depth author profiles and interviews, excerpts of the hottest new releases, literary games and contests, and a lot more with readers every week. They even have an on-going contest where teens can win a TeenRead tote bag full of newly released books.

(www.teenreads.com). For those with kids under age 13, check out www.kidsreads.com. There is even a www.20somethingreads.com for you guessed it, 20 year olds.

Swap Books?

Have old books you've already read? Try swapping. There are several online sites that will allow you to trade/swap books with other readers for FREE. Some sites even allow members to trade CD's, DVD's and video games. Please check details because you may be responsible for shipping costs on some sites. Here are few to get you started:

www.titletrader.com
www.paperbackswap.com/index.php
www.swaptrees.com/swap_books.php

Too Many Books?

If you need a little extra cash try selling your gently used unwanted books.

Half Priced Books is a resale chain bookstore. Simply bring your items in for a quote. You can either get in store credit or cash. (www.hpb.com)

The better deal is to seek out privately owned "mom and pop" shops. Smaller shops tend to pay a little more for items then chain stores. Shop around for the better quote.

Of course there is always selling on-line. Two of the most popular sites are Amazon or Ebay. Another great site is www.bookscouter.com. Bookscouter is a free website that compares book buying sites to provide you with the highest buyback price.

Aspiring Author?

Looking for a little help getting your best seller up and running? Try Groupon for some great deals on writing courses and equipment. You need to create a log in and indicate what state you're in for local deals. I'll explain more about Groupon the site later on. (www.groupon.com)

Where to Find?

Check your local libraries for in house programs and national programs. School systems often provide details of featured reading programs in school newsletters and flyers.

Family magazines and book centered publications often advertise programs with larger sponsors. Check bookstore information boards, tables, and checkout. When doing an online search, be sure to be specific and check reviews before using. Last but definitely not least, ask friends and family about what they are utilizing. A trusted opinion goes a long way! And check reviews before using. Last but definitely not least, ask friends and family about what they are utilizing. A trusted opinion goes a long way!

ANIMALS & STUFF

The FREE offerings at the zoo are out there, but are not quite as easily found as with some other venues. Occasionally they offer FREE admission. Check their website, local publications, and listen to your local radio station for details. There are a few websites out there that have a list of zoos all over the country that offer free admission. Check out the following list of zoos that offer free admission all year round:

www.trekaroo.com
www.aza.org/free-admission

Check into your local Zoo's volunteer program. Each program is different and may offer opportunities for participants as young as 14 years old. This is a great way to not only get into the zoo for FREE but also learn about and work with the animals.

The Indianapolis Zoo does offer FREE admission to children ages one and under. Also, if you are a true animal lover an annual pass is pricey but provides unlimited admission all year long, FREE admission to special events and discounts to other services. The membership will pay for itself within 2.1 visits for a family of four.

The Bronx Zoo does offer a donation admission on Wednesday. In essence you could pay less than the regular admission price. Certain local financial institutions offer FREE admission to account and cardholders. (www.bronxzoo.com)

The Cincinnati Zoo offers Visitor Appreciation Days with 50% off admission. (www.cincinnatizoo.org)

The Humane Society is a great place to give animals some one on one attention. There are various volunteer programs available mainly for 16 years and up. They also have youth and summer programs starting at ages 10 and up. In Indy there are Parent & Me Days that allow families to volunteer together. There is still an age requirement of at least 8 years old. Check the main and your local site for details:

http://indyhumane.org/index.php/get_involved/volunteer_opportunities

www.humanesociety.org

State Fairs can be another option to check out some animals. The Indiana State Fair is filled with plenty of livestock to see and pet. During the days the fair is open The Indianapolis Star newspaper usually runs a full-page ad on the back of the Healthy Living section for a FREE one day admission ticket to the fair. They never announce what day they will print the ticket. Luckily, it is usually spread by word of mouth. There is a State Fair directory equipped with dates and locations. The site provides direct links to each location which can be searched for deals and FREEBIES. (www.ncstatefair.com)

Animal themed amusement parks like Sea World and Busch Gardens tend to cater any FREE options to special individuals. Military staff will always have some type of discount and occasionally FREE admission. There are always timeshare presentations for FREE tickets to the major parks.

Note that timeshare companies usually require a major credit card to sign up for the presentation and can often take lengthy amounts of time out of a day to hear the pitch. Representatives can often be very pushy if you do not purchase their vacation time.

Where to find?

Local radio stations and newscast's are great sources for finding out about FREE zoo options. Zoos tend to put the word out at the last minute to control crowds. Still check websites for last minute posts. Most stations have websites and broadcast live events often. Radio Disney usually has a spot at many of the kid friendly events around town. You can find a local station at radiodisney.com or just ask your child, I'm sure they would know! Also check the community calendar of local news stations.

Low income families can usually find free or very low cost tickets and even low cost annual passes through government assistance offices.

MUSEUM & HISTORY

Now you may have thought the museum was just a boring place with old paintings, but it is actually a haven for wonderful FREE and fun things to do. Here is a list of some popular museums around the country.

Did you know that the Metropolitan Museum of Art (www.metmuseum.org) and the American Museum of Natural History (www.amnh.org) in New York City function on suggested admission prices? This means that you can pay any price you want for a ticket to the museum. Just go to the admission desk and ask. I have heard that the desk attendants can be a bit pushy towards making you pay the suggested admission price. Note that if you are not able to pay it that you can stress that you can only donate what you have and you should NOT be denied admission.

The Indiana Museum of Art in Indianapolis offers FREE admission every day. Special exhibits cost but the rest of the museum is FREE to roam. They have plenty of interactive exhibits for kids also. Check out the Garden Walks on Saturdays and Sundays. This walk is a FREE guided tour through IMA's gardens. In early May the Starlite series begins which entails free art-making projects inspired by works of art in the IMA's permanent collection. If you check with the information booth, they will be sure to inform you of any other FREE events going on in the near future.

NOTE: In early 2015 the IMA decided to start charging admission in the amount of $18 per adult, $10 for children 6-17, and annual family memberships at $55. If you attend or work for a university or grade school, check your benefits. You may have FREE or low cost options available to you. (www.imamuseum.org)

If you are in the windy city, Chicago, check out the Adler Planetarium. This famous attraction offers several FREE admission days through out the entire year. The Chicago Children's Museum has FREE admission every first Monday of the month for children ages 15 and under. If you are a resident and own a library card, you can check out a Kraft Kid's Museum Passport at any Chicago public library. The pass is checked out just like a library book but must be returned within a week. The pass is valid for up to 4 admissions into about 12 different cultural attractions in the city.

www.adlerplanetarium.org
www.chipublib.org/

Now the best kid's museum on earth is our very own Indianapolis Children's Museum. They host several FREE days throughout the year. The first Thursday of every month is FREE admission to the public. Indiana residents receiving government assistance can obtain $1 admission cards valid for entry into both the Children's Museum and Connor Prairie. (www.childrensmuseum.org)

Target Stores take pride in supporting the arts. Target sponsors FREE or reduced priced performances and museum admissions all over the country. Target's website is the best place to find out about a FREE or reduced price event near you (https://corporate.target.com/corporate-responsibility/community-events)

Some of the best moments in history come in smaller packages. The IPS Crispus Attucks Museum located in the Crispus Attucks High School in Indianapolis glorifne of the first all-black schools in the state of Indiana. The museum showcases many accomplishments, along with famous over-achievers that have walked the halls from day one to today. Though there is a small admission fee, the museum offers FREE tours Monday through Friday from 9am to 4pm during summer months. (www.crispusattucksmuseum.ips.k12.in.us)

WHERE TO FIND?

Local utilities often are sub-sponsors of art events in the city. Read the inserts that come with your bill. Neighborhood specific newspapers and community segments on local news programs are great resources to find out about anything regarding the arts. Museums usually play a big part in the communities they are in, so also check small business for community boards and posted flyers in near-by neighborhoods and state tourism sites. Free and low cost annual passes are another thing for low income families to check into at their local benefits office. Government workers, teachers and military employees usually have great discounts available to them also. Check your employee benefits department.

FUN IN THE PARK

Not only is just visiting a local park site FREE, they also offer a lot of other FREE activities to fill your days.

I think most public parks in every city show FREE movies in the park. The parks usually offer more family friendly choices. There is nothing like an outdoor movie experience, especially if you live in a town that no longer has a drive in theater. Bring a blanket and snacks for a great fun filled evening. Be sure to check for restrictions on the types of food and drink allowed. There may be options to purchase items on site also. Government & public park centers/websites will have information on times and locations. (www.usa.gov/Agencies/State-and-Territories.shtml)

Central Park in New York City holds an annual Summer Stage series of concerts all summer long. Major artist preform for that's right, FREE! (www.summerstage.org)

Los Angeles Department of Recreation and Parks offer FREE programs for youth ages 5-18. LA Kids provides FREE sports programs and classes throughout the year at their 100 locations. (www.laparks.org/lakids/index.htm)

Check out Summer on the Canal at the Indiana Historical Society (IHS). Starting late May every Thursday from 6-8pm, enjoy a FREE concert on the lawn of the canal. You can enjoy the canal and good sounds at no cost.

Beginning at dusk on Fridays in August and September, the IHS also participates in Movies in the Park. They usually show the older black and white flicks. This makes for a romantic evening or just a night out with the family. (www.indianahistory.org)

There are several festivals throughout the summer that usually have FREE admission where you can at least listen to good music and there are children's activities to participate in. Here are a few in Indianapolis.

• In late June, the annual WFYI's Let's Meet PBS KIDS in the Park is held at Veterans Memorial Plaza/American Legion Mall in downtown Indianapolis from 10am to 4pm. Children of all ages can come meet, greet and interact with the characters that are featured on the PBS network. There is plenty of entertainment and engaging educational activities to keep little one's busy all day all for FREE. (www.wfyi.org/events) The greatest thing about PBS is that they have kid's festivals in many states. Check your local PBS station's website for information.

• Eagle Creek Park, 7840 West 56th Street, hosts the All American Kids Fishing Derby in early June for ages 4-14. This is a FREE event, however registration is limited. Call the park office at 317-327-7116 for more details. This event is national event. The best way to search via the internet is by your city and the title of the event.

WHERE TO FIND?

The beauty about most parks is that they also serve as an information center. Most parks have centers that offer places for people to relax and/or participate in sports, exercise, or fun activities. Also check travel centers, state government websites, public park websites (specific to your city), local newspapers ,and the city tourism websites. The links below are directories for most parks within the US. Major events are usually showcased on the home page.
www.americasstateparks.org/Find-A-Park
www.great-kids-parks.com

FESTIVALS

Most festivals are seasonal and are usually held in the spring and summer months. If you volunteer to work for a festival, you can usually receive FREE admission. In some cases children may volunteer also. Some festivals offer free credit for whatever they are showcasing. For example, the 2009 Indianapolis Broadripple Art Fair offered credit towards art classes for volunteers along with free admission and an event T-Shirt. Here are a few that could be worth the visit.

Have a great love for art? Check out www.artfaircalendar.com/. This website lists top Art/Craft fairs throughout the U.S. This site can also provide details on the shows, blogs, ways to contact artists and ways to get your personal artwork in a fair.

If you're in the Midwest check out the Stutz Business Center on 10th Street. This Indiana historical site is the home to several artists of all media types that host various receptions, classes, and gallery events throughout the summer for all ages. The building has its own association and website www.stutzartists.com.

The Annual Indian Market, also held around mid to late June, is a cultural event you won't want to miss. There is an adult admission but children are FREE and the adult admission price includes entry into the Eiteljorg Museum. It is a unique journey into the traditions, food, and artisans of the Native American culture. To find similar events around the country, check out Pow Wow calendars and events at www.powwow.com and http://www.discoveramerica.com/

At the Talbot Street Art Fair, there is not an admission price view at over 200 artist booths. This is a historic area street fair where you can browse booths of local artist.

IDADA (Indianapolis Downtown Artists & Dealers Association) First Fridays is a moving tour of local artists. The group showcases all mediums of art in different galleries and museums around the city. It is an elegant affair for all lovers of art. (www.idada.org)

Search for First Friday events in your state through your state's tourism website.

I stumbled onto the Tourism Fair one day during a lunch break. Even if you don't have plans to travel within the state, the vendors offer FREE promotional items. You can load up on FREE crayons, pens and pencils, notepads, and cups that will keep your children amused for hours. Look at your cities tourism website and AAA for details on upcoming tourism fairs. (https://autoclubsouth.aaa.com/events/travel.aspx)

Don't forget about the local library. I once attended a book signing where a famous comedian's mom spoke and local artist performed. The admission was FREE and it was a half-day of great entertainment. Libraries host many festivals and free events for the community.

Check out your state's government website. Find the link for happenings around town for a great source on FREE festivals and concerts in that city.

WHERE TO FIND?

Let's start with a national website for art fairs around the country, www.artfaircalendar.com. Art Fair Calendar can keep you up to date with the future fairs coming up in almost any state. Most museums work together to support each other and will post information on upcoming fairs on their website and at the information desk. If you know what neighborhood the fair will be in, more often than not that neighborhood has a website and an association office. These neighborhood associations take great pride in the events that occur on their streets so they will have plenty of marketing materials at local businesses and even print their own newspaper or magazine. Street newspaper dispensers are great places to look for festival events.

FLEA MARKETS & SALES

Is finding a bargain more your cup of tea? Flea Markets/Sales also offer FREE admission for volunteers. Just Between Friends is a consignment sales event that caters to children's and maternity items. It usually runs over a weekend at a fairground facility. All the items come from small business owners or individual families with gently used items. It's a great place to get low cost items for new moms and children. All unsold items are usually donated to a local non-profit organization. The best thing about this group is that that they have sales all over the country. Check jbfsale.com for more details.

Consignment and resale shops are all over this nation. It's an easy way to sell gently used items if you don't have time for a garage sale. There are plenty of options that offer resale designer items. Search resale shops in your city online to find the closest one.

A popular option is online consignment stores and subscription boxes. Online stores sell handmade or gently used items through cyber network. They usually don't have a physical store location. These items can vary in pricing so shop around for the best price. A few popular sites are:

www.thredup.com
www.Therealreal.com
www.Poshmark.com
www.Liketwice.com

Subscription boxes are handpicked curated items in every category possible that are shipped once a month. From makeup to workout clothes to things geeks love. You name it. There is a subscription box for it. I like them because you can try things you would like to sample first before dishing over the full price. There are a lot of affordable options that offer some great products. No matter how much the box is, the contents are retailed at 50-60% higher than what you pay for it. A lot of the companies offer either a FREE first box or extremely discounted first box. Many customers post YouTube unboxing videos where you can see what comes in a typical box and what that customer thought of each item. Here are a few list websites that will give you plenty of options:

www.mysubscriptionaddiction.com/
www.cratejoy.com
www.subscriptionboxes.com/

Go shopping for antiques, crafts, furniture and more or just take a browsing walk through the Woodruff Place Flea Market. This event usually occurs over a weekend in early June. Woodruff Place is located east of downtown Indianapolis between 10th and Michigan Streets. Enjoy 80 acres of bargains, food and entertainment. For more information call 317-627-8982 or www.woodruffplace.com.

WHERE TO FIND?

Great flea market locations are usually found in your major local newspaper and housed at your local fairground facility. Some of the smaller locations will be posted in regional periodicals. There is a directory site to check most major cities, www.findafleamarket.com. Depending on how big it is, you may hear radio spots for the event. In my town we have a huge marquee in front of the most popular location for the bigger flea markets. That marquee will display details of the next upcoming sale. Also check fairground and convention center websites for a list of events, as flea market sales are often held in these types of locations.

http://flea-markets.find-near-me.info/
www.swapmadness.com/

Resale and subscription stores are mainly online Consignment shops are usually located in historic or college areas. Do an online search for locations in your city.

SPORTS AND GOOD TIMES IN THE SUMMER

What is Indy's best kept secret on great finds in the summer? The McCoy Book – (Marion County Commission for Youth) www.mccoyouth.org/youth-activity-directory.html is a valuable resource not only for summer camps but also for programs and groups supporting the youth of Indiana, many of which are FREE. You can find many resources through this website. This 12 year old non–profit funded by United Way provides a comprehensive list of youth services and programs. There is also The Easy Book, which can be downloaded from their site that is geared towards low-income families that are looking for resources to assist in all aspects of life. Yet this book has plenty of options for any family dynamic. Check out United Way's website for options for your city.

Summer free lunch programs are often offered in most major cities. Their focus is to ensure all children get at least one healthy meal a day. They service all of the community. Serving sites are mainly in public parks and community centers. Check your state's public park website and your local community center for details.

Do you have little entrepreneurs on your hand? Try Prepared 4 Life's Lemonade Day competition. Lemonade Day is a free, national initiative designed to teach kids from grades k-8 on how to start, own and operate their own lemonade stand business. This program was created by Indiana native Scott Jones to encourage youthful entrepreneurship. Visit the website or one of the program's sponsors to register and receive a FREE backpack with all the details on how to get started. This is a one day event where participants can earn income or donate to a charity that participates in competitions of achievement. Check out the website or visit your local library. NPR, National Public Radio, is also a sponsor for this event. (www.lemonadeday.org/)

Radio and sports personalities host youth enrichment programs usually in their home town. While in attendance of a kid's street fair, my son won a free week long session at professional basketball player Bonzi Wells' Basketball Camp. Steve Harvey has a foundation that dedicates time to mentoring young males from grades 8-11 for a weekend during Father's Day. Registration can be found at http://smharveyfoundation.org/programs/

If selected, the organization will fly the young man and one adult to Dallas, TX for a weekend of mentoring for FREE. Qualifications include that the young man be raised in a single parent household without a father figure present and must live in one of the 48 contiguous United States and Washington, DC (excluding Alaska and Hawaii).

His wife has a female version, Girls Who Rule the World. Information can be found at the site above.

The Harvey's also host the very competitive Disney Dreammaker's Academy weekend at Walt Disney World in Florida. It's an intense long weekend of career enrichment for high school students. (www.disneydreamersacademy.com/be-a-dreamer/apply)

The Kids Bowl FREE Program at Royal Pin Leisure Centers is a great campaign that is trying to pull families into local bowling alleys for the summer. Families from coast to coast receive two FREE bowling games every day during the summer. Simply register each child in your home at www.kidsbowlFREE.com/royalpin. There are even family passes available for adult members for a fee.

Local bowling alleys usually team up with schools and aftercare programs to distribute coupons to be used during school breaks. Most offer at least one free game of bowling.

Ever participate in a program at your local Girl's Inc., Boys and Girls Club or local community center? If not now is a good time to sign up. Not only do these organizations offer several FREE programs and events, once you join them at one of them you are forever on their mailing/email list. You may ask, isn't that just more junk mail? Well, it would do you well to read through that correspondence. My kids have attended FREE seminars, sporting events and even received

FREE merchandise as part of attending sponsored events. Usually the club either receives donations or has a budget to purchase tickets to various family friendly events. They offer tickets to their members and participants in their programs. These are also good volunteer opportunities for adults and teenagers.

www.girlsinc.org
www.bgca.org

Public parks and large churches usually have the lowest cost sport programs for every age. My son participated in a basketball league at the age of five. Some of his teammates were as young as four. One of the largest sport programs in Indianapolis is held at Tabernacle Presbyterian Church at their recreation center. Tab offers low cost options for anyone wanting to participate in just about every sport thinkable. Tab often provides FREE equipment that the children get to keep.

www.tabrecreation.org
www.findlocalparks.com

Where to find?

A lot of these suggestions came from word of mouth sources. Word of mouth can be a golden source of great programs. Whoever tells you about a great program usually has taken advantage of it and has received some benefit from it. NPR (National Public Radio) is also a great source of national programs and local public service programs available in your city. Their radio programs are syndicated and broadcast all over the country. So please check the website for your local station. (www.npr.org)

Outreach programs hosted by celebrities are showcased on that celebrity's website. Many athletes host youth camps and programs.

Community center information desk and materials are great resources for free and low cost summer fun. Always ask about what they have to offer. Library information tables/areas can also be a valuable resource. Thoroughly look through material available and only take what you need. Librarians will likely only know about events specific to their branch.

The best places to look for bowling deals are in your kid's backpacks. Schools are eager to support organizations that support them. Almost all schools host an all-class-grade skating party at different times of the year. And the locations offer coupons to get that return business. Check the bowling alley itself. Just like libraries, bowling allies have flyers located in the doorway and/or the front desk with all their feature promotions. This information is there for a reason and you might miss out if you don't look.

To find out about FREE offerings at your local Boys and Girls club or Girl's INC, look in local parenting/kid focus periodicals, or simply visit a location and ask what they have to offer. These groups are always looking for people to participate in their programs so they will welcome your inquiry.

CRAFTS & HOBBIES

How many times have you walked into a Lowe's or Home Depot just for home improvement concerns? I bet you thought all they do is sell home improvement products. Well think again.

Several hardware stores offer how to classes for children and adults. The courses are usually available on weekends from FREE to low cost. Schedules for classes are available at the service desk or the store website.

It's not just hardware stores that offer classes for children of all ages. Check out fabric and craft stores. Try the links below for a few places to start.

www.lowes.com
www.HomeDepot.com
www.joann.com
www.michaels.com
www.hobbylobby.com

Simon Mall Properties, owner of major malls all over the country as well as Canada, Japan and Malaysia, offers a low cost program for young children called Simon Kidgits Club®. Parents can sign up their kids online or at the Mall's service center for a $5 fee. Children receive a T-Shirt and membership card along with invites to mall promotions and activities. Recent activities have included a FREE chef set along with activities for making fun nutritious treats and Radio Disney concerts just to name a few. Parents can also receive special offers for shopping discounts in the mall. For more details and to view their interactive web activities check out: www.simonkidgitsclub.com

There are some great crafting subscription boxes available. Half the fun is getting that box of surprises every month. You won't know what projects are included in each box until you receive it. This is a great way to learn new techniques. Check out these few suggestions to get you started:

www.darbysmart.com/
www.baribox.com

Where to find?

Just about every hardware store and craft store has classes for all ages. Inspect their offerings well. You may find more FREE options than you think. Check with your local mall information booth for details on kids' clubs and other offerings. Advertising for these events are subtle and they usually rely on the traffic in the mall on the date of the event. That mall information booth has a lot more to offer than just directions.

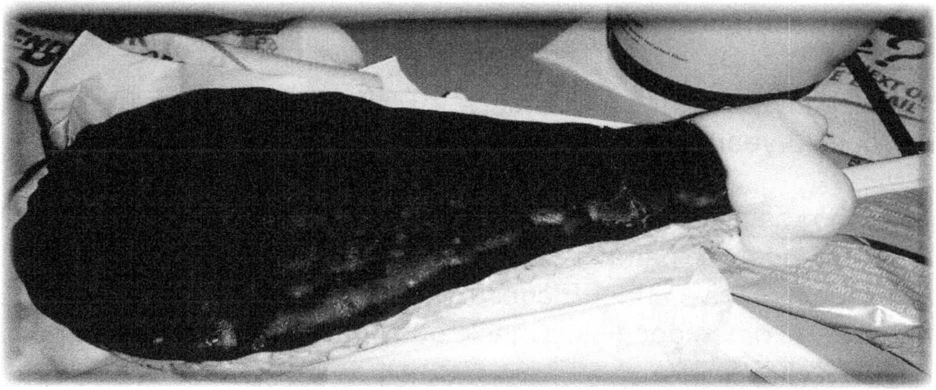

GOOD EATS

There is nothing like FREE food. I found this fantastic website: http://www.mykidseatfree.com

The site allows you to search by state/city to find local restaurants that offer kids eat FREE nights. You can strategically plan to feed the kids with a free meal offered by several different restaurants. Some deals may require a purchase. Make sure to read all of the details listed. Parenting magazines are good places to search. Also, if you do an online search of your city's name plus "kids eat free", you should get a decent list of local eateries.

Another way to get a FREE meal is to visit the website of your favorite restaurants or any restaurants you may wish to visit. Many places are now offering FREE appetizers or FREE entrée's for special occasions (birthdays/holidays). Here are a few more options and details:

- FREE meals for your birthday.... IHOP encourages customers to join their Pancake Revolution. IHOP will send registered patrons a coupon for a stack of three FREE pancakes on their birthday. The site will allow parents to sign up a spouse and all children in the household. (www.ihop.com)

• Denny's will give customers a FREE Grand Slam breakfast. Anyone 13 years of age and older can sign up at www.dennys.com.

• Who knew that you could get FREE food from Barnes and Noble? For kids under 13, parents can sign them up for the B & N Kids' Club. Recipients receive a FREE cupcake from the in-house café and number of other goodies. Check out https://kids.barnesandnoble.com/kidsclub/

• Live out on the west coast? Black Angus offers a FREE steak for your birthday with the purchase of a second entrée of equal or greater value when you join their Prime Club. Locations are limited so check to make sure there is a restaurant in your town or a town you are visiting at the time. (www.blackangus.com/primeclub)

• Join the Red Robin email list and get a FREE burger plus a gift at sign up for your special day. You have to pick up a FREE Red Royalty card from any one of their restaurants and register it on-line to sign up. (www.redrobin.com)

• Baskin Robins and Cold Stone Creamery both have birthday clubs that offer a FREE scoop on your special day. They both also allow you to add family members to your one registration.

www.baskinrobbins.com
www.coldstonecreamery.com

All You magazine has a webpage dedicated to all things you can get FREE for your birthday or any day. Some of the offers are samples that come with coupons and some items are some pretty nice things. (www.allyou.com/free-on-birthday)

Public events can be a snack haven. Vendors and field marketers target outdoor festivals to pass out FREE samples and coupons for FREE food/drink items for local retailers. If you are already at a particular event, check out the vendors passing out information. Many times you can get a good treat and maybe a FREE lunch for you and your kids.

How many times have you watched the TV show Extreme Couponing and thought I wish I could do that. Extreme couponing takes a lot of patience and time. You can still take advantage of some of the benefits on a smaller scale.

Have you ever paid attention to those grocery coupons that print with or on the back of your receipt? I used to leave those extra coupons that print at the self-check out at the register. Well that was

until one day I took one and it was for a FREE 20 oz new beverage. Don't leave any stone unturned. Coupons are back in style.

My local Kroger grocery store even offers coupons for discounts when purchasing certain items. They usually post a sign in front of the product in red writing stating that if you buy one or more you can get a coupon for a few dollars off your next grocery bill. What I do is buy those items first, get the coupon to print, and use the coupon on the rest of my items. Great way to increase your savings!

Grocery email blasts usually offer free items once a month with no additional purchase required. Sign up on their website. You can now also add e-coupons to your grocery rewards card. The discount is automatically applied to purchases when the card is scanned at checkout. (www.kroger.com)

There are plenty of online coupon and rebate apps that make it easy to save on your grocery bill. One of my favorites is www.ibotta.com. It is a grocery rebate site. It allows you to make purchases online, in store and link reward cards for instant cash rebates. Once you accumulate a certain dollar amount a check or direct deposit can be made to your bank account. It's FREE to sign up and a great way to earn extra cash. Checkout51.com is another similar application. Both allow you to use a smart phone or tablet to rake in the dollars. You can combine savings with coupons. The rebates are verified with a copy of the receipt.

I don't know about you but I love fresh produce. On Wednesday, from the month of May through October, the Indianapolis Farmer's

Market comes to Indianapolis City Market in downtown Indianapolis. Various farmers in Indiana come to sell fresh produce and handmade products from 10am to 1:30pm weekly. Located at 222 East Market Street, for details call or email: 317-634-9266 / www.citymarket@indycm.com. Most cities have Farmer's Markets. With the boost on healthy living several groups are working together to offer more and more locations.

One last resource that can't go unmentioned, for you culinary lovers, Basil Magazine. www.basilmagazine.com. Chef V. De'Vonne Williams has created an on-line magazine dedicated to good food. She has great articles for all ages, along with reviews of cooking tools, a radio streamed show, and a chance to win some great prizes. I was fortunate enough to win a cheese grater that is absolutely fantastic.

WHERE TO FIND?

Best places for FREE eats are signage in the restaurant or grocery store and their websites. Parenting and women magazines such as All You, always have great coupons for food items or national chain eating places. (www.allyou.com)

To find Farmer's Markets all over this country, www.localharvest.org is a great website to use. The site also highlights festivals relating to farms and harvest.

Food magazine and networks are great sources for contest, ideas, and national events. I like looking for foodie bloggers or extreme couponing bloggers. They will offer great information and great contests with better chances of winning than national companies. The best way to find blogs is by doing a defined search specific to what you're interested in. Example: top Italian food blogs.

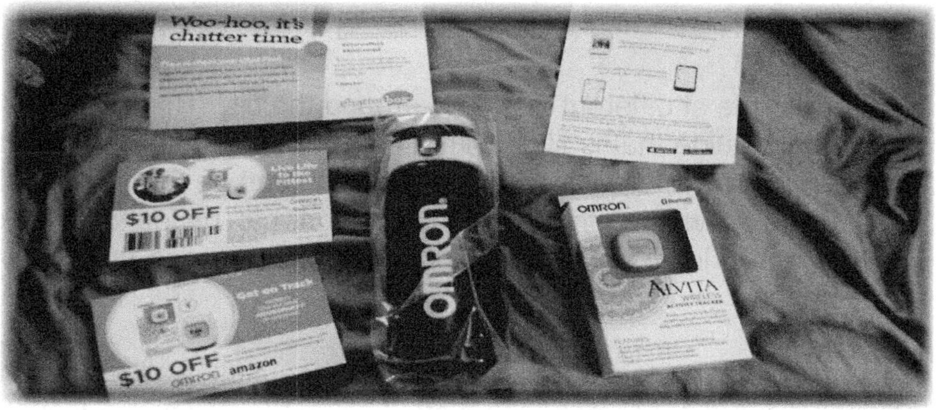

GET FIT

The first place to look for fitness deals is your employer. You can often get a major discount or fantastic deal on fitness plans through employer benefits and insurance. A division of Blue Cross Blue Shield offers a super discounted fitness program that offers access to several gym chains across the country for a low fee and sometimes with no initiation fee. They also have a point system that allows you to earn points for reading health and fitness information and for each visit to the gym. The points can then be redeemed for prizes like luggage, appliances, gym equipment, and even clothes. The best way to find out if your insurance offers something similar is to check the website thoroughly. Unusually you would have to log into your account to get access to the information. If you can't find it call your insurance provider and ask.

Also check your company's EAP(employee assistance program) benefits. Through my company's EAP benefits, we can get discounts on major attraction tickets, movies, warehouse memberships, and more. If you are having trouble finding information ask your human resource department. These benefits are part of your hiring package and there for you to utilize.

My local park and recreation system, Indy Parks, usually has

FREE gym time at different locations around the city. They publish a season park guide that is filled with all of the available programs at the different park sites. This FREE publication can be found at local libraries and anywhere other FREE publications can be found. Check with your city's local park and recreation system to see what they have to offer.

Have you ever looked at your city's beautiful walkways? In Indianapolis, the public can take a stroll along the downtown Canal. There are many locations to access the canal. It has a scenic natural trail that leads all the way behind the zoo one direction, and towards urban city areas in the other direction. There are interactive outdoor displays as well as natural seating which is great for picnics and lush biking routes. Plus, this is a great way to get good exercise in that everyone can enjoy. Every city has locations usually close to parks or museums that anyone can enjoy for FREE. Take a walk and check it out!

The Indianapolis Museum of Art (IMA) offers a FREE walk through the IMA garden daily during the summer months. This is a great way to get in great exercise and gaze at the beautiful array of flowers. Check your local museum of art. They take great care of the area surrounding the property and often offer FREE self walking tours.

Ever thought that you might need to get tested for an illness that runs in the family? Clarian Health holds FREE health screenings at various locations all over the city. This is a great opportunity to get several FREE health tests for common serious diseases/illnesses. Check the website for the current FREE screening schedule: www.clarian.org/

Many hospitals offer or sponsor free health testing. While some are focused on low income families, a lot of programs are for anyone who is interested. Most of the funding is for informing the public regardless of their financial situation

Having a baby or is someone in your family expecting? Get a free Graco Pack n Play. All you have to do is take a sleep class that teaches about the most up to date ways to safely put your newborn to sleep and prevent SIDS. The program is offered all over the country and anyone expecting or child care providers can take the class to get the crib. I took the class with my mom and we both received the pack n play along with a sleep sack and other goodies. These same organizations offer other free and low cost baby items. (www. cribsforkids.org/find-a-chapter/)

Subscription boxes are another great resource. Graze and Love with Food are two great low cost options. They are both $10 and under per a month. They offer a variety of healthy snacks to try once a month. These are just a few. Check the subscription box list site mentioned earlier for more options.

www.graze.com
www.lovewithfood.com

WHERE TO FIND?

To find fantastic FREE fitness options, start with your company's insurance website. The insurance company will often showcase events sponsored by participating health organizations covered by that network. (www.bcbs.com)

Check local hospital websites for a list of events. Each major hospital has at least one FREE event every year. Check with the service desk at your local gym for any current programs. They are loaded with information of FREE community events. Healthcare is a huge push at these types of events.

Doctor's offices and clinics will also have plenty of information about free and low cost services. The best way to get information is to ask for it. Physicians have access to information on lots of things that are free to clients. My doctor's office offers free mammograms.

For walkways and park offerings visit local park information centers or take a look at your state government website.

MOVIES GALORE

Earlier, I mentioned the FREE movies available at public parks and libraries. Those are just a few ways to catch a flick around town.

Most major theater chains offer a FREE or low cost summer movie series for kids. Shows usually start early in the morning on certain week days and seating is on a first come-first served basis. There are also options for children with sensory issues.

Regal/United Artist Cinema offers a Regal Crown Club rewards card where you can earn points toward FREE movie tickets, popcorn and candy.

AMC also has a movie watcher program similar to Regal/United Artist Cinema.

www.regmovies.com/Crown-Club
www.amctheatres.com/amcstubs

Did you know that most on-line movie rental companies offer FREE trials? The FREE trials usually last for at least 30 days. When you sign up, the most popular allow you to build a list of desired rentals. The first rental on your list is mailed to your address within a few days. The quicker you return your movie after viewing the quicker you will receive your next request on your list. There are a few things to look out for:

- Some services require a credit card to sign up.

- You have to remember to cancel the membership within the trial period if you don't wish to continue the service.

Red Box kiosks are normally located in front of various locations, which include: McDonalds, Wal-Mart and Kroger locations. These rental boxes offer current video rentals for just $1 a day and now they also offer video game rentals. If you sign up for their online newsletters you can earn a FREE rental on a monthly or weekly basis. The best thing about any of these rental box options is that you can return the video to any box location anywhere. That means if you travel you can check locations on line to return videos watched on the road. The airport even offers a similar video box option that may be a little pricier but check the online options for free rentals. (www.redbox.com)

Netflix is still a popular online DVD rental company. They now allow streaming of rentals through gaming systems and computers. This feature makes movie viewing very easy, without the hassle of driving to pick up a DVD or waiting for it to arrive in the mail. (www.netflix.com)

Want to see movies new to theaters? Check out your local newspapers and radio stations. Premier showings occur often. Local papers usually advertise either contests, that offer FREE movies or first come first serve tickets. One year we saw every newly released film in the summer. Sign up for the website newsletters which will notify you of contest or special offers including movie tickets along with many other goodies. Most of these sites are now working off a point system and some allow you to earn points for gifts by viewing their advertiser's websites. Here are a few places to start:

www.nuvo.net
www.indy.com

Another way to get access to FREE movie screenings are websites dedicated to finding free screenings in your city. Search by zip or city for current available screenings.

www.advancescreenings.com
43KIX is a Facebook page
www.gofobo.com

One last FREE movie watching option that can't go unmentioned is your local library. This is a great option for FREE DVD rentals. The library usually has a great current movie selection. If they don't have a movie you would like to see, you can request them to purchase the DVD to put into circulation. Beware that you will be charged a fee for late returns but there is no fee to check out a DVD just like a book. (www.publiclibraries.com)

Where to find?

Newspapers and magazines are the best places to look for FREE movie deals. The entertainment sections of newspapers and special features of magazines often list premieres and info on FREE rentals. Visit the information table at your local theater or even the information desk/ticket counter. There is always a table with flyers and information regarding the theater. I found out that theaters host birthday parties much like restaurants, just by looking at the flyers.

TRAVELING BARGAINS

With the high cost of flying, driving to a vacation spot is the next best thing. Auto Driveaway is a car relocation service. You can sign up to drive cars to owners/dealerships that have relocated to other cities for FREE. To sign up you must be at least 23 years old, have a valid driver's license and good driving record. There is a required, but fully refundable $350 security deposit. Considering you would pay that much for a rental car even if flying to/from your vacation spot, this is one better since it is fully refunded once delivery is complete. Once your approved you will be supplied a car with a full tank of gas, an appropriate amount of days and miles to complete your trip. (www.autodriveaway.com/driver)

Want to visit the greatest place on earth? In 2009, Disney offered FREE admission for any visitor on their birthday. In 2010, Disney offered FREE admission to one park by volunteering through the "Give a Day Get a Disney Day" program. With a little research you can find the deal of the century. If you volunteer for any of the many races held in the parks, you can earn free admission to the parks, snacks or apparel. (www.rundisney.com/volunteer)

Disney has continued servicing the community with the community. The most recent opportunity is mainly available for in state patrons, but if you're in town during the event, it could be a great possibility.

The ESPN Wide World of Sports has an option on its website to volunteer for various sporting events at the facility. Different events earn points toward FREE admission to a Disney park. Please see website for each events date and eligibility:

www.espnwwos.com/volunteer-opportunities

Disney is very expensive but can be done on a budget. The best way to get started is with Disney Vacation Account. The account allows you to set a budget over a period up to 5 years. There are no penalties and it can be funded with credit, debit, direct deposit and even Disney gift cards. A credit or debit card must be linked to the account initially to get started. No funds need to transfer into the account until you are ready or you can just fund with gift cards after the initial set up. A full refund can be requested at any time. The biggest benefit is that for every $1000 you spend on your vacation, you are eligible for a $20 gift card up to a total of $500. The online access allows you to track your progress, set goals and provide support when needed. To further add to your discount, purchase Disney gift cards from Sam's club with a savings of $7.02 per a pack of three $50 cards then deposit into your vacation account. You can also purchase discounted Disney gift cards from Target using the 5% savings with the Target Red Card.

A second option is to use official discount brokers for cheaper tickets. I've only dealt with brokers in Florida but I'm sure they are available in areas with numerous attractions in place. Be sure to check reviews and that the broker is an official seller before purchase. My favorite for Orlando attractions is Undercover Tourist. They offer discounts on the major and popular attractions and dinner shows in the area. They also often offer a deal where buying so many days qualifies for a free days admission.

www.undercovertourist.com
https://disneyvacationaccount.disney.go.com/
http://www.samsclub.com/
http://www.target.com/redcard/main

Military staff can receive numerous discounts & FREEBIES from the Walt Disney Corporation and many other entertainment/attraction.

Check the website for the latest offers:

https://disneyworld.disney.go.com/special-offers

Thoroughly investigate all options available to military staff.

One of my favorite Disney related websites is a must do. It's a blog called Couponing to Disney. The blogger has made this wonderful site with the main goal of saving money to take a Disney vacation. The best thing about it is she has comprised a comprehensive list of deals that will simply help you save on just about anything you can think of. Not to mention a good number of FREE offers and chances to win some great prizes. She has an email blast that you can sign up for and two Facebook group pages. This site can be a great tool around the holidays too. I won a $100 Disney gift card that I was able to use towards a Disney vacation. This site is one you should definitely check out whether you are going to a Disney location or not! (www.couponingtodisney.com)

My favorite Disney podcast that must be mentioned is WDW Radio run by Lou Mongello. This guy left his lawyer gig on the east coast to move to Florida and report on all things Disney. He's written a bunch of guides and information books about hidden deals within the parks on how to save money on a vacation. He also posts YouTube videos. He has a deep passion for Disney and provides great useful information. (www.WDWRadio.com)

There is a large community focused on everything Disney and everything Universal and ... I hope your starting to get my point. Disney is a place I love but if you love Universal or Kings Island or whatever the same benefits listed above can be applied across the board. The best place to get started for information on your favorite destinations is to search for blogs and podcasts. There are plenty and they all have information on how to get there on a budget.

Here are a few options to choose from to get you started:

www.mousesavers.com
http://kicentral.com/
www.thecoasterguy.com/

Interested in international travel on a budget? Here are two options to make travel across borders easier. The first is more for single people with little obligations or responsibilities but if you do a thorough search you may be able to find a company to accommodate a single or married parent. Teaching English abroad is on the rise all over the world in non-English speaking countries. There are several companies that recruit Americans and a teaching license is usually not required. This is one option that could have a salary attached depending on the length of the contract. Many companies require at least a year commitment, though there may be shorter options to assist with workshops. Make sure you check to see what a company will pay to get you in a classroom. You could end up with most, if not all of the entire transportation and lodging paid for. Check out GoAbroad.com & the Hess Educational Organization to get started.

www.goabroad.com
www.hess.com.tw/en

Another way to travel abroad is through a volunteer travel program. These programs do require that you pay for your travel, yet non profit organizations have very low cost options available due to the nature of the trip. Expedia has a separate division dedicated to volunteer vacations, which they call VolunTourism. Visit www.voluntourism.org/ to investigate this travel option. There are blogs and resources on how to make a great vacation meaningful. Travelocity even offers a grant to help pay for your stay at http://svc.travelpn.com/TravelForGood/index.html

There are several agencies to help with the details.

Where to find?

Large companies like Disney launch national campaigns. They will have plenty of commercials, radio spots, and large full-page ads in major publications. Some of the hidden deals will come from those small articles in magazines, newspapers, podcasts, blogs and from how to articles or books like this one. All amusement parks should have some type of volunteer opportunity available. For popular places, opportunities will fill up fast.

One thing I always do when I'm visiting any place other than home is check out the local visitor's bureau. There is so much information to be found here. The employees are usually extremely helpful with any questions you may have and they almost always offer some type of discount card or FREE deal for coming in.

Www.charityguide.org/volunteer/vacations.htm is a great site for international travel whether volunteering or teaching.

FOR MORE DETAILED WAYS TO SAVE ON TRAVEL,
VISIT MY WEBSITE:
WWW.JUSTASKKIKY.COM

POINT CARDS & APPS

We all have to purchase groceries and gas. Most of the major grocery chains offer shoppers cards that allow you to not only take advantage of in store discounts but some can accumulate points toward things like discounts on gas, frequent flyer miles, or discount on in-store services.

Speedway Gas has a great point plan that allots points just for purchasing the gas you need anyway. I like to buy a $100 Speedway Gas card and use it with my speedy rewards card. This way I can budget my gas and get extra points for buying the gas card. Points can be redeemed for everything from merchandise in the store to various gift cards and savings on gas.

CVS issues Extra Care Bucks when you make a certain dollar amount of purchases over a certain period of time. These extra bucks are like in store credit that can be used toward the purchase of any merchandise in the store. Download the CVS app and get instant $5 Extra Care Bucks. Download the app via ITunes or Android App Store.

Some of my favorite websites for point cards:

www.speedway.com/SpeedyRewards

www.cvs.com
www.marsh.com
www.kroger.com

Make sure to check the fine print on the frequent visit card. Some businesses require certain purchases in order to accumulate points

Upromise.com is a great site to earn money to pay off a student loan or save for a college education. It is FREE to sign up. The site will request you register your debit/credit cards along with any point cards and some gift cards. When you use any of these cards on selected items, those retailers and companies agree to donate a percentage of that sale to your Upromise account. You can apply the accumulated balance to a savings account, student loan, 529 college savings plan or request a check. It is small amounts that can add up quickly. They have online shopping options to increase your savings by purchasing what you would anyway but through their site so they can use a code to get the donation.

If you fly a few times out of the year, check out Points.com. They have an extensive list of frequent flyer programs and hotel stay programs that you can register your account in their FREE membership program. Points.com will keep track of your various points and offer ways to swap and trade for accumulation in one program to get your travel reward or even to use on their very own retail rewards. Please check the site for details. There may be costs associated with trading or swapping points.

My most favorite point app, or rather kicks app, is called Shopkicks. Download this trendy app and get "kicks" for simply walking in stores. Sign up for FREE. For the app to work properly the locater on the smart phone must be enabled. Shopkick uses the locater to pick up signals connected to the stores speaker system that will award kicks when the app is turned on when walking into one of the designated retail locations. Kicks can also be accumulated by scanning products, in store purchases, scanning through product pages and inviting others to join. Kicks add up quickly and can be used to redeem for gift cards or luxury items.

I've redeemed my kicks for gift cards that I was able to apply to a vacation. I love this app. It is the easiest way to earn FREE gift cards with no obligation or personal information required. Download the app via ITunes or Android App Store. (www.shopkicks.com)

Where to find?

Just about every retailer and restaurant has a point/discount card. The best place for point cards are in the store itself. If you belong to any of the point accumulation sites, they will have links to sign up for cards on their websites. A lot of stores are also incorporating apps to make it convenient to sign up and manage the account. Look for signage in the store indicating additional savings for downloading the app and/or signing up for text messages.

Another fantastic place to get info on the latest money saving apps and cards are retail savings related blogs and podcast. I mentioned Couponing to Disney earlier. They do a fantastic job of keeping their members on top of the latest saving vehicles available.

Understand that there are a huge amount of apps and point cards available. Be sure to determine if the benefits fit your needs before signing up. You do allow retailers to send advertising to you when signing up.

JUST FREE STUFF IN GENERAL

The next few chapters are ways to get some FREE stuff in general. They don't take you out of the house, but FREE is FREE. I can always use FREE useful things. Also this section includes FREE things that many of my friends and family often ask me about. So take a look at what you can find for FREE.

FREE Stuff On-Line

Walmart truly is the place where you can find everything. On Walmart.com there is a FREE sample page full of things to try through the mail. The site is updated often and can offer anything from diapers to pet food. Target.com also has a FREE sample page. Take a look to see what you can find!

Feminine product companies are always offering FREE samples of their newest products. Check out the website of your favorite brand or check the box for the headquarter address to snail mail a request for any samples available.

Got close friends and relatives in another area code but short on the cash to reach out and touch? Skype and FaceTime offer a FREE service that allows you to place FREE long distance calls over the internet. With a webcam you can see your caller too!

Do all your friends have unlimited texting yet it's a bit much on your plan? www.pinger.com/ is an app that will send text messages to any phone for FREE.

Pandora.com is one of the best radio apps, in my opinion. The app will allow you to type in a song title or artist and will select music based on your selection that is in the same genre. At least for me the selections are dead on. Give it a try. There are few others that can also be accessed on smart phones including Slacker Radio. Check with your cell provider app store for more details.

Just want FREE stuff, check out All You Magazine on line. This site is great. Not only do they provide some great ideas for ways to save money and great advice for families, they also provide one of the best FREE sample giveaways ever. Often you can get full size FREEBIES from major retailers. I've received everything from hair products to detergent. There are some really great finds so don't skip this site! (www.allyfrom ou.com)

P&G has a great website filled with high dollar coupons, great ideas on how to use their products and contests. (www.pgeveryday. com)

MONEY

Did you know that the IRS has established a group called VITA, Volunteer IRS Tax Assistance, to assist with filing your taxes for FREE. This group can be accessed via the IRS or at satellite locations like local libraries and community centers. Once you get the help and you want to file electronically but still need it to be relatively cheap or FREE, go to www.irs.gov. The website lists companies that will file your return electronically for FREE as long as your AGI qualifies.

Check all the details because there may be other stipulations to qualify.

When I decided to return to college after many failed attempts, I didn't qualify for much financial aid and I didn't want to get a loan. When I lost my job it was a curse and a blessing at the same time because it provided the best opportunity for me to pay for my education. An Individual Development Account (IDA) is the best thing since sliced bread for low income families. The way it works is that participants must sign up for financial asset building classes and open a savings account with a specified banking institution over a period of time. Every time a deposit is made the government matches the deposit 2/1 and sometimes 3/1. The requirements are that you must be within a certain income guideline specific to the state and you can only use funds for buying a house, education (college or private secondary school for kids) or starting a business. Withdrawals do have to be approved. I was able to fund my college degree with this program. Every state's requirements are different, so don't rule yourself out. I always say try first. All they can say is no. (https://cfed.org/programs/idas)

Looking for extra cash?

Try Ebates.com. This site is a cash rebate program. Do your regular shopping on line through this site and earn cash rebates. That equals money back in your pocket. Combine rebates with discount codes to get the maximum benefit. There are restrictions per each retailer. Be sure to read the fine print. As an added bonus for new subscribers, earn an automatic $5 bonus rebate. (http://www.ebates.com/rf.do?referrerid=Pu8XIVF8GARmP6G6%2Ff7hQw%3D%3D&eeid=26471)

Since I joined www.e-rewards.com less than a year ago, I have been able to acquire two major gift cards just by completing online surveys. It's worth taking a look. Surveys are designated dollar amounts that add up quickly to be exchanged for gift cards to major retailers like Target or can earn travel miles/points or FREE subscriptions to popular magazines.

LOOKING FOR AN AT HOME OR PART TIME JOB YOU CAN DO FROM HOME?

Look no further than www.workersonboard.com/
I stumbled on the YouTube videos and later joined the Facebook group page. This is one of the most extensive list and reviews of online work from home jobs resources available. The woman that runs the company has tried just about every opportunity so she can verify it's legit.

THROW A PARTY!

Houseparty.com allows anyone to sign up to host branding company sponsored events. If you love having at least 10 or more guests over for a fun time, check this site out.

The way it works is that the potential host creates an account which will allow them to apply to host a party focused on a new product, hit TV show, or a great cause. You do have to be selected to be a host for a particular party. Don't worry. There are several types of events to choose from. The selected hostess then receives a box full (see examples below) of all the goodies/FREEBIES needed to throw a big "shabang" and promote the sponsor's product. Houseparty.com has opportunities for all ages. (www.houseparty.com)

WHERE TO FIND?

I find a lot of quick FREE sites in parenting and women magazines. I'm sure there are some in men's magazines also. Look for those small one or two paragraph articles usually on a page with about five different topics. Check large retailer websites like Walmart and Target for samples and even their non-profit pages. There is usually great stuff there.

Get acquainted with the podcast and blog circuit. There is an overload of information here to find all things such as the ones listed above. There are also groups that focus on how to extreme coupon using these sites by combing offers. Leave no stone unturned!

JUST THE BEGINNING

These are just a few things to get you started. Be sure to check public bulletin boards and FREE publications. For all you web based folks. Many sites have links to partners that may offer great opportunities. The possibilities are endless.

I hope you are able to find a few things to keep you and your loved ones busy. And remember to keep your eyes and ears open for additional activities! And if all else fails just ask me!

KIKY
JustAskKiky@gmail.com

RESOURCES

Library & Reading Resources:

www2.scholastic.com
www.20somethingreads.com
www.bookadventure.org
www.bookscouter.com
www.groupon.com
www.hpb.com
www.kidsread.com
www.paperbackswap.com/index.php
www.publiclibraries.com/
www.swaptrees.com/swap_books.php
www.teenreads.com
www.titletrader.com

Zoo/Animal Interest Resources:

www.aza.org/free-admission/

The Wildlife Conservation Society
2300 Southern Boulevard
Bronx, New York 10460
(718) 367-1010.
www.bronxzoo.com

buschgardens.com

www.cincinnatizoo.org
3400 Vine Street
Cincinnati, Ohio 45220-1399
(513) 281-4700 or (800) 94-HIPPO
info@cincinnatizoo.org

www.humanesociety.org/

www.indianapoliszoo.com
1200 W. Washington St. Indpls., IN 46222
(317) 630-2001

indyhumane.org/index.php/get_involved/volunteer_opportunities
www.ncstatefair.com
www.seaworld.com
www.trekaroo.com/

Museums & Cultural Sites:

Adler Planetarium
www.adlerplanetarium.org
1300 South Lake Shore Drive
Chicago, IL 60605
Telephone: (312) 922 7827

American Museum of Natural History
www.amnh.org

Chicago Public Library Kid's Passport
www.chipublib.org/

Crispus Attucks Museum
www.crispusattucksmuseum.ips.k12.in.us
Indiana Historical Society

450 W Ohio
Indianapolis, IN
www.indianahistory.org

Indiana Museum of Art
4000 Michigan Road
Indianapolis, IN
www.imamuseum.org

Metropolitan Museum of Art
www.metmuseum.org

Target Sponsored Community Events
https://corporate.target.com/corporate-responsibility/community-events

The Chicago Children's Museum
www.chicagochildrensmuseum.org
700 East Grand Avenue
Chicago, IL 60611-3577
(312) 527-1000

The Children's Museum
www.childrensmuseum.org

The World Museum Community
www.icom.museum/vlmp/usa.html

Park & Recreation Resources:

www.americasstateparks.org/Find-A-Park
www.findlocalparks.com
www.golosangeles.about.com
www.great-kids-parks.com/
www.indianahistory.org
www.indygov.org

Los Angeles Department of Recreation and Parks
www.laparks.org/lakids/index.htm

State Government Website Directory
www.usa.gov/Agencies/State-and-Territories.shtml

www.summerstage.org

PBS Kid's Indianapolis
www.wfyi.org/events

Festival Resources:

www.artfaircalendar.com/

AAA Travel Fairs
https://autoclubsouth.aaa.com/events/travel.aspx

www.discoveramerica.com/

Indianapolis Mass Ave Tourism Website
www.discovermassave.com

First Fridays
www.idada.org

www.powwow.com
www.stutzartists.com

Flea Market Resources:

www.cratejoy.com
www.findafleamarket.com
http://flea-markets.find-near-me.info/

Just Between Friends Consignment Sales
www.jbfsale.com

www.Liketwice.com
www.mysubscriptionaddiction.com/
www.Poshmark.com
www.subscriptionboxes.com/
http://www.swapmadness.com/
www.Therealreal.com
www.thredup.com
www.woodruffplace.com

SUMMER PROGRAM RESOURCES:

Boys & Girls Club of American
www.bgca.org

www.disneydreamersacademy.com/be-a-dreamer/apply/
www.findlocalparks.com
www.girlsinc.org
www.kidsbowlFREE.com/
www.lemonadeday.org
www.mccoyouth.org/youth-activity-directory.html
National Public Radio
www.npr.org

Steve Harvey Foundation
http://smharveyfoundation.org/programs/

www.tabrecreation.org

CRAFTS & HOBBIES RESOURCES:

www.baribox.com
www.darbysmart.com/

www.lowes.com
www.HomeDepot.com
www.joann.com
www.michaels.com
www.hobbylobby.com
www.simonkidgitsclub.com

Good Eats Resources:

www.allyou.com
www.allyou.com/free-on-birthday
www.basilmagazine.com.
www.baskinrobbins.com
www.blackangus.com/primeclub
www.citymarket@indycm.com
www.coldstonecreamery.com
www.dennys.com
www.ibotta.com
www.ihop.com
www.kids.barnesandnoble.com
www.kroger.com
www.localharvest.org
www.mykidseatfree.com
www.redrobin.com

Get Fit Resources:

Blue Cross Blue Shield Insurance
www.bcbs.com

www.clarian.org
www.cribsforkids.org/find-a-chapter/
www.graze.com
www.lovewithfood.com

Movies Galore Resources:

www.advancescreenings.com/
43KIX is a Facebook page
www.amctheatres.com/amcstubs
www.gofobo.com/
www.indy.com
www.netflix.com
www.nuvo.net
www.redbox.com
www.regmovies.com/Crown-Club

Travel:

www.autodriveaway.com/driver
www.charityguide.org/volunteer/vacations.htm
www.couponingtodisney.com
https://disneyvacationaccount.disney.go.com/
https://disneyworld.disney.go.com/special-offers
www.espnwwos.disney.go.com/about/volunteer/
www.goabroad.com
www.hess.com.tw/en/
www.JustAskKiky.com

Kings Island Central Blog
http://kicentral.com/

www.mousesavers.com
www.rundisney.com/volunteer/
www.samsclub.com/
www.target.com/redcard/main
www.thecoasterguy.com/
http://svc.travelpn.com/TravelForGood/index.html
www.undercovertourist.com
www.voluntourism.org
www.WDWRadio.com